Lucy Maud Montgomery: STORY GIRL

Alexandra Kay Power

Basswood Hill Books

Text and illustrations ©2024 by Alexandra Kay Power

Hardcover ISBN 979-8-9867855-8-5

eBook ISBN 979-8-9867855-9-2

This book is an illustrated biography for young people depicting Lucy Maud Montgomery's youth. Illustrations for this book were created using watercolour pencil.

TABLE OF CONTENTS

Early Years _ _ _ _ _ _ _ _ _ _ _ _ 1

School Days _ _ _ _ _ _ _ _ _ _ _ 11

Teen Years _ _ _ _ _ _ _ _ _ _ _ _17

Early Adulthood _ _ _ _ _ _ _ _ 25

Marriage and Literary Success _ _ 35

Works Cited and Consulted _ _ _ 40

Acknowledgments _ _ _ _ _ _ _ _ 43

About the Author _ _ _ _ _ _ _ _ 45

For Madeline

EARLY YEARS

On November 30, 1874, Lucy Maud Montgomery was born in Clifton, which later became New London, Prince Edward Island, Canada.

Montgomery's birth place

She was 21 months when she came to live with her grandparents, Alexander and Lucy Macneill at their homestead in Cavendish, Prince Edward Island.

Macneill Homestead

Her grandparents were in their fifties and all their children were grown. Their youngest daughter, Emily, remained at home. Lucy Maud's mother, Clara Macneill Montgomery, had recently died of tuberculosis. Maud's father, Hugh John Montgomery, left to go west to Saskatchewan not long after her mother died.

Maud, as she was called, had a high forehead and slightly hooded eyelids. She had a small mouth like her mother, Clara, thick brown hair, and blue eyes. Maud was small and slim in her body size. She was smart, imaginative, she spoke well and had a lot to say.

Maud at 8 years

She had a couple of imaginary friends, as some children do, whose reflections she saw in the glass doors of a bookcase at home and to whom she chatted at length.

She had many playmates in the village, some of whom were relatives. They would play together outdoors at the nearby seashore, wading in the water, collecting pebbles and climbing the sand dunes. She also liked to go strawberry picking up by a maple wood.

Sandhills in Cavendish

Max and Topsy

According to *The Selected Journals of L.M. Montgomery*, Maud had two cats when she was a child, Max, "a gray, Tiger-striped fellow", and Topsy, "a motherly old gray-and-white " (1: 13). One day, Topsy followed her to her prayer meeting, and hid under the church (1:3).

She also liked to walk in the woods around the village. Her favourite path was a shaded spot with ferns, wildflowers, a babbling brook, and scented evergreens. She named it "Lovers' Lane" and referred to it many times in her journals and it appeared in her books. "Haunted Wood" was what she called the dense pine forest where she would go to scare herself when she felt like it.

Lovers' Lane

During the winter months all would gather in their warm kitchen, where her grandfather would tell stories. The family kitchen also served as the village post office.

Macneill kitchen

Although the backdrop for her childhood seemed ideal, her home life could be troubled. Her grandfather was moody and sometimes sharp tongued with her. Maud was a sensitive child and she learned to be observant of others' facial expressions and emotions. Grandfather Macneill was intelligent and a good storyteller, though. It was from him that Maud acquired her ability to string a yarn.

Her grandmother was a good housekeeper, very proper and sometimes strict. Maud always knew Lucy loved her, though. Maud attended the Presbyterian church, sometimes with her Aunt Emily.

Grandmother Macneill

SCHOOL DAYS

When Maud began school at six years old, the teachers realized right away that she was very bright. When she read aloud, her first teacher, Mr. Ross, declared that she could read better than any of the other children, even though she was younger and had never been to school.

Schoolhouse in Cavendish

Her next teacher, Mr. Fraser, would award good work or behaviour with prizes, such as books, which he bought with his own money, and Maud ever after remembered him kindly.

Maud had an excellent memory and was able to recite stories that she read. Though she had few listeners in her own household, she had many friends and relatives, with whom she often played the role of "Story Girl," a name which later became part of the title of one of her books, *The Story Girl*. She read widely from magazines, religious works and fiction, such as *Little Women* by Louisa May Alcott.

Maud's grandmother wasn't her only female role model. A new teacher, Hattie Gordon, arrived in Cavendish when Maud was fourteen. Miss Gordon made school fun, and Maud thrived under her teaching.

Hattie Gordon

Maud didn't like arithmetic, but enjoyed composition, and wrote a piece on Cleopatra. She began to keep a journal of her daily activities. She continued to do so for the rest of her life, and eventually, her journals were published. She read widely and she found many more role models in the books she read.

The more Miss Gordon praised her writing and reciting talents, the more Maud wanted to become an author and to obtain a higher education. Miss Gordon asked her to recite in a poetry reading, along with her school chum, Mollie. Another friend, Nate, was clever and intellectual, and together they liked to talk about books.

She traveled to Park Corner where Silver Bush, the home of her Campbell cousins, Aunt Annie and Uncle John, was located. She visited them often in her youth. The Campbell home was a favourite of Maud's.

Her cousin, Frederica or Frede Campbell was a kindred spirit and close friend, particularly when they were young adults. Frede would die young, at the age of 36 years, in 1919.

Frederica or Frede Campbell

TEEN YEARS

At Park Corner, she not only visited Silver Bush, but also the home of her Grandfather Montgomery, or "Grandpa", as she called him, whom she loved more than her Grandfather Macneill. He was a senator. She met Sir John A MacDonald, the Premier of Canada, who was a great friend of his, and who was touring PEI at the time.

Grandpa Montgomery

A pond at Park Corner, "Lake of the Shining Waters" as Maud refers to it in her journals, was favourite spot of her youth. It was also featured in *Anne of Green Gables* as a cherished location of the main character, Anne Shirley.

Lake of the Shining Waters

Maud was sixteen when she went to stay with her father and his new wife for a year in Prince Albert, Saskatchewan. She was dazzled by the Prairies which were filled with bluebells and other flowers. She thought the house was lovely. She met her stepmother and little half-sister Kate.

Maud's father

Maud saw love in her father's brightly shining eyes and felt very fond of him, after a long and very hopeful separation. He smiled with pride when Maud showed him her first published poem. She had secretly sent it into a periodical.

She didn't feel the same way about his wife as time marched on. According to Jane Urquhart in her book *L.M. Montgomery*, Mrs. Montgomery showed signs of a temper and asked her dad not to call her "Maudie" because she felt it was too childish. Mrs. Montgomery insisted that Maud drop out of school to do housework and care for the new baby, while she went out to socialize. On one occasion, she didn't bother to pour tea for her, and Maud found her to be cold and rude (Urquhart, 13-14).

She made friends with Edith Skelton who was hired by the family as household help. It turned out that Edie didn't much like Mrs. Montgomery either. Not long after Maud arrived, Edie was sent home.

After her stay, she traveled by train to Toronto and Ottawa, where she visited her Grandpa Montgomery again. Because he was a senator, he worked in Ottawa. She saw the Parliament Buildings, the Library, and witnessed a session in the Senate with him.

Maud returned to Cavendish, though she didn't want to leave her father. Nine years later, he died. Throughout her life, she remembered him with love, and projected some of that affection onto the male characters in her books (Urquhart, 15).

Her childhood in Cavendish was lively and adventurous and she thought of that home fondly ever after. Cavendish was the inspiration for the village of Avonlea in Maud's Anne books.

EARLY ADULTHOOD

In the summer of 1893, she wrote her entrance exams for teachers' college in Charlottetown. In August, she heard of the passing of her Grandfather Montgomery. He had been ill for a long while.

She returned to Cavendish, and as she ambled through Lovers' Lane, she took great comfort in her surroundings. She wrote in *The Complete Journals of L.M. Montgomery: The PEI Years, 1889-90*, "Apart from its beauty, I have a strange love for it. In those divine woodland solitudes one can hear the voice of one's own soul — the voice of nature — the voice of God" (165).

Lovers' Lane

She passed her exams and her Grandmother MacNeill drove her to Prince of Wales College in Charlottetown in the fall. Soon after she began to study there, she had another poem published in *The Ladies World* in New York. When she graduated the following spring, she was chosen to speak at the ceremony.

She had trouble finding a teaching position, but eventually found one in Bideford, where she taught for a year. She earned almost enough money to attend Dalhousie University in Halifax, Nova Scotia. Her grandmother, Lucy Macneill, made up the difference.

She continued to send poems and stories to periodicals to have them published. Three pieces met with success in early 1896 and she enjoyed seeing her name in print.

She returned to Cavendish that summer and then went on to another teaching position in Belmont, where she stayed with the Simpson family. She developed an interest in Edwin Simpson, two years older, handsome, intelligent and talkative.

Edwin Simpson

Ed, as she referred to Edwin Simpson, began to express his love for her, and she accepted a marriage proposal from him. Though she had her doubts, he reminded her of happy times at Park Corner, where she had spent time as a child. She returned to Cavendish. She continued to write and sold more of her work during that time.

In fall of 1897, she moved to Lower Bedeque, where she stayed with the Leard family. There she was drawn to Herman Leard, who was open, good natured, and funny. She felt like he appreciated her personality more than Ed, who was more self-absorbed. In early spring, she realizes she wants to break off her engagement with Ed.

She returned to Cavendish in March 1898 for her Grandfather Macneill's funeral when he died. Then she traveled back to Lower Bedeque briefly to finish her teaching term. Her romance with Herman Leard ended when she went back to Cavendish. He died the following year of complications from influenza.

She had settled into a routine with her grandmother, where she wrote constantly, and her grandmother would perform the household chores. Though she wasn't making a lot of money with her writing, she was making progress. She was happy to be home, and enjoying her life in Cavendish.

When she heard the news that her father had died of pneumonia in January 1900, though, she took it very hard.

Maud as a young adult

In the fall, someone she knew from Dalhousie University, who worked for the *Halifax Echo* newspaper, recommended her for a position as a proofreader and journalist, and she got the job. She moved to Halifax, but very quickly grew homesick. She chose to return a year later.

MARRIAGE AND LITERARY SUCCESS

Ewan Macdonald

In September 1903, Ewen Macdonald, or Ewan as she wrote of him in her journals, arrived to serve as minister at the Cavendish church.

Five years later, she published Anne of Green Gables, her most successful novel, during a very promising period in her life. She had met and befriended Ewan, her future husband. They had entered into a secret engagement. The novel would win international acclaim. She wrote numerous sequels to it in the years to come.

After her grandmother died in 1911, she married Ewan. They had three sons, though the second didn't survive childbirth. Maud was deeply affected by this loss. During the following period, the wars caused her great anxiety as well.

She would go on to write and publish more than twenty books, and many more short stories. There were also poems, nonfiction, journals, letters, and essays. She was also a frequent public speaker.

Maud died on April 24, 1942. According to the family doctor, the cause of her death was a nervous illness, from which she had suffered for some time. In any case, the circumstances surrounding her death left it unclear. Upon her death she returned to her cherished home of Cavendish, PEI to be buried.

In 1923, Lucy Maud Montgomery was the first Canadian woman to be accepted as a member of the British Royal Society of Arts. She was honoured by King George V as an Officer of the Order of the British Empire in 1935. She was also elected to the Literary and Artistic Institute of France. The Canadian Federal Government named her a National Historic Person in 1943.

WORKS CITED AND CONSULTED

L.M. Montgomery Institute. "L. M. Montgomery." University of Prince Edward Island, accessed January 21, 2024

lmmontgomery.ca

McIntosh, Andrew and Cecily Devereux. "Lucy Maud Montgomery." The Canadian Encyclopedia, 2022, accessed February 28, 2024

thecanadianencyclopedia.ca

Montgomery, L. M. Anne of Green Gables. William Collins, 2022.

_____. Emily of New Moon. McClelland and Stewart, Ltd., 1925.

Reid, Catherine. The Landscapes of Anne of Green Gables. Timber Press, Inc., 2018.

Rosenberg, Liz and Julie Morstad, ill. *House of Dreams: The Life of L.M. Montgomery*. Candlewick Press, 2018.

Rubio, Jen, editor. *L. M. Montgomery's Complete Journals: The Ontario Years 1911-1917*. Rock's Mills Press, 1916.

_____. *L.M. Montgomery's Complete Journals: The Ontario Years 1918-1921*. Rock's Mills Press, 2017.

_____. *L. M. Montgomery's Complete Journals: The Ontario Years 1926-1929*. Rock's Mills Press, 2017

Rubio, Mary Henley and Elizabeth Hillman Waterston, editors. *The Complete Journals of L. M. Montgomery: The P.E.I. Years, 1889-1900*. Oxford University Press, 2017.

_____. *The Selected Journals of L. M. Montgomery, Volumes 1-5*. Oxford University Press, 1985-2004

Rubio, Mary Henley. *Lucy Maud Montgomery: The Gift of Wings*. Random House of Canada Limited, 2008.

_____. "Montgomery, Lucy Maud (Macdonald)." Dictionary of Canadian Biography, Vol. 17. University of Toronto/ Laval University, 2003, accessed February 28, 2024

http://www.biographi.ca/en/bio/montgomery_lucy_maud_17E.html

Urquhart, Jane. Extraordinary Canadians. *L. M. Montgomery.* Penguin, 2009.

Watercolours portraying Montgomery, her friends and relatives, and special places are based on photographs in the L. M. Montgomery Collection (Photograph Collection call # XZ1 MS A097 Boxes 1-7). Archival & Special Collections, University of Guelph.

ACKNOWLEDGMENTS

Many thanks to Mary Henley Rubio, who was my Children's Literature professor many years ago at the University of Guelph, for her scholarly biography, *L. M. Montgomery: The Gift of Wings*.

Also. thanks to both Rubio and Elizabeth Hillman Waterston for their combined effort in editing *The Selected Journals of L. M. Montgomery, Volumes I -V*, which I discovered and read when I traveled to PEI one summer, and which sparked my interest in Montgomery to begin with.

More recently I found and read *The Complete Journals of L. M. Montgomery the PEI Years 1889-1900*, also edited by Rubio and Waterston. My intent was to create a book which would focus on Montgomery's youth for young readers.

Thanks also to Jane Urquhart for her biography on Mongomery which I also read and from which I gained further insight.

I am grateful to Jen Rubio, as well, for her edited works, *The Complete Journals of L. M. Montgomery the Ontario Years*, which I also read a number of years ago and provided background knowledge for the book.

Also many thanks to Curtis Sassur and Melissa McAfee for giving me access to the photographs in the L. M. Montgomery Collection at the University of Guelph, and to Melissa for being so helpful.

Finally, thanks to now retired librarian, Cecile Hastie, and teacher, Pam Pletsch for looking over the manuscript. Also, thank you to Ademir Kalač and Fiverr for his design and tech work, without whose help this book might not be possible.

ABOUT THE AUTHOR

Alexandra Kay Power was born and raised near Ottawa, Ontario. She has written and illustrated five picture books for children. This is her first biography for young people.

www.ingramcontent.com/pod-product-compliance
Lightning Source LLC
Chambersburg PA
CBHW040732060526
44119CB00078B/286